ALL SORTS

Written by
Bruno Bouchet

Illustrated by
Richard Hughes

GREEN CANDY PRESS

Published by GREEN CANDY PRESS
San Francisco, CA
www.greencandypress.com

Copyright ©2003 Bruno Bouchet and Richard Hughes
Originally published in Australia by Hodder Headline Australia

ISBN 1-931160-19-8

Interior design: Yolanda Montijo
Editor: Kevin Bentley

PRINTED IN CANADA BY TRANSCONTINENTAL
MASSIVELY DISTRIBUTED BY P.G.W.

All Sorts is dedicated to all those who think they *may* be in the book, those who *know* they're not, and especially to Chris, who can stack my bottom shelf anytime.

Perspex Closet

The denizen of the Perspex Closet thinks no one at work knows he's gay. The fact that he flounces into work in gorgeous suits, drinks Diet Coke, has a week off after Gay Pride every year and was the only bloke invited to Sharon from reception's girls' night seems irrelevant to him because, after all, he is straight acting. To him the biggest compliment that could be paid is for someone to say, "Really? I had no idea you were gay!"

He jealously guards his see-through closet door—when he remembers. He can't appear in Gay Pride Parade in case someone from work sees him but he somehow forgets his colleagues when the community photographer turns up at a dance party to snap him and a couple of cute guys. When a picture's printed he runs to his friends proudly showing the photo and declaring with almost convincing concern, "I hope no one from work sees it."

Being in the Perspex Closet is no hindrance to organizing his social life at work and he thinks his colleagues don't notice that the only people who call him are Dave, Andrew, Mark and David. A few different men leave messages on Monday mornings, but never get called back. When asked, "Who was that?" he always replies, "Oh, just a friend". His colleagues are saddened by this—they wish he could find a nice boy and settle down. ✳

3 am Queen

There is a moment at any dance party, usually around 3 a.m., when suddenly the world is a lovely place full of beautiful people. One of those beautiful people is Jason. Be careful not to let him kiss you before he takes his Chupa Chup out:

"Look, I know we've only been dancing here for a few minutes and I'm off my tits but this isn't the drugs talking, I'm not that out of it, I never am, I always know what's happening and what's real or not, and this is real. I've seen you before ... somewhere ... and I've always really, really admired the way you have such a good time ... wow look at those lights, they're amazing, just sooo blue ... it was at the gym. I see you at the gym and I really, really respect the way you work out. God I love this track I've never heard it before but it's just the best. I could swear they played the theme from *Charlie's Angels* before, sounded just like it ... but what I really, really wanted to say is, want some chewy, do you know what the time is, don't the clocks go back tonight or something? But seriously I just wanted you to know that I love you, honestly I love you." ✷

3

Musical theatre is alive and well in Australia as will be proved by a visit to any inner city café where magnificent performers can be seen at their finest:

"OK what'll it be then ... Angela, hi darls, haven't seen you since *Cats* in Brisbane, 'Daylight I will wait ...', never got to sing it on stage but I've made up for it in here. Had much work since then? I had a forty worder on *Passions*—a clinical psychologist bringing back Miguel's memory. Forty words from me and it all came flooding back. I got a callback for *Sunset Boulevard*, one week before it closed. Then I was all set for chorus plus Hugh Jackman's understudy in *The Boy from Oz*, but he couldn't stand the competition - one look at my *I Go to Rio* and I was out. Then my agent had me up for some miserable PBS nuclear testing in the Pacific drama but I was supposed to speak French, and knowing all the lyrics to 'Voulez Vous' didn't count. Did get promised a few lines in the Les Mis comeback but the thought of trudging round on that dreary revolving stage all over again practically had me in a rash.

"What? Oh the blades. Two words for you, darls: *Starlight ... Express*. Isn't it fabulous, Halle-Lloyd-Weber-lujah! The old team back together. We knocked spots off the London cast according to that producer that came out. Anyway mum's the word or every waiter in town'll be strapping on roller blades and hurling lattés over the customers." ∗

5

American Tourist

American visitors in Sydney for Mardi Gras can be spotted by their gleaming straight white teeth and the standard issue "I'm gorgeous enough to be one of Tom Bianchi's friends" body. Of course as soon as they land on Oxford Street, they are smothered in attention and surrounded by cooing locals. The smart ones realize that boys are more interested in laying hands on their addresses than on the contents of their Calvin Kleins. The dumb ones end up with lots of Australian houseguests in June.

Jetsetters on the world party circuit, they are determined to savour the Earth's rich variety, sample different cultures and explore new ways of life as they traverse the globe in lycra shorts. A United Nations of Dance, they groove to the same music with the same men all around the world. It's White Party, Black and Blue, Ibiza, Aspen and then on to Sydney for Mardi Gras. After a week's recovery in Far North Queensland, they head back to the States to design their bodies for next year's circuit— "calf implants are going to be big". Then they resume their normal lives of ignoring all the guys they said hello to because they were in a foreign country and prepare for the onslaught of Sydney visitors. ✶

8

The Lesbian Match-Maker

Although Jan completely accepts the validity of a non-relationship based lifestyle for Brett and acknowledges his right to view casual sex as a fulfilling and rewarding encounter, she still wishes he could find the happiness she's found for the last twelve years with Freda.

Brett himself is not totally opposed to having a boyfriend, it's just that Jan makes the mistake of assuming personality is what makes men attractive. She likes to think that people who are beautiful on the inside are beautiful on the outside, regardless of their looks. Brett does not agree: he hasn't spent the last three years torturing his body at the gym just to pick up guys on the strength of personality.

"Brett, you should meet this guy who's started working at the rehab center. He's really nice ... no he doesn't go to the gym but he cycles to work sometimes so I think he's quite fit ... well he tends to wear loose clothing ... I haven't looked at his crotch, it's not my area of expertise. But he's really cute, gets on well with dykes, loves French and Saunders and he's vegetarian. You'd like him if you got to know him ... I think he's good looking. He's more interesting than those gymbots you normally pick up. He's really smart, he's doing a master's on queer identities ... I don't know why you're making such a fuss – the amount of time you spend in back rooms, you've probably had him already!" ✳

Queer Artist

Nik walks barefoot through the streets of Newtown with his mongrel dog on a scarf masquerading as a lead. He rejects notions of sexual pigeonholing and is uncomfortable with the terms Queer and Artist. He fears the word Queer prohibits him from being accepted as what he really is—a "worker–explorer on the boundaries of sexual freedom." The word Artist is burdened with centuries of bourgeois pretensions. He's not here to make pretty things, but to create powerful statements that cause the maker's distorted view of the world to impact on the viewer's equally distorted perception, in full knowledge that the journey from artist to viewer irredeemably alters the work each time someone views the piece.

Nik's latest exploratory mission is a collage of penises photocopied from porn magazines: "I deliberately set out to confront and confound and so some penises were enlarged and some shrunk, some from so-called 'straight' porn and some from 'gay' porn, so ultimately the notions of straight, gay, large, small are totally annihilated. I've included my penis because as a worker–explorer I feel trapped by the world's attempt to define me sexually and this is my act of breaking free. It's called 'Suck This: Explosions From a Pigeonhole Terrorist.'" ∗

Art Queen

"Darling of course I'll be at the Moët launch—oh really, you were invited too—marvellous! Now, you are coming to the Mittelman opening ... mmm yes red and white, we'll be serving both.

"What did you think of the MCA opening? Yes, I agree, very dull. Now if only they had Absolut as sponsors again it would have been vodka and cranberry juice all round and a good time had by all. As it was, it was so boring I ended up having to look at the art on the bloody walls.

"So when are you coming into the gallery ... mmm Friday might be tricky, it's a full schedule. I've got the wine people in at eleven. We're changing the Semillon for openings ... yes I know, everyone's serving it now so we've got the merchant in to sample something new. Then Bill and I are popping out for lunch with Patrick, the caterers are in at four to discuss next week's dinner function ... sorry sweetheart, you can't – it is a very exclusive dinner ... that's the day pretty much sewn up I'm afraid. Next week I'm off to Melbourne for a quick scoot round Christie's.

"Why don't you pop in Saturday morning, it'll have to be early though ... yes eleven o'clock, fine. Listen I'll have to go, I've got Liz due in at any moment and I'm hoping she'll bring Michael— I want him for one of my openings. Ciao!" ✳

13

Bouncer Model

Vinnie isn't actually gay, he's just a straight gay club bouncer whose girlfriend stays home a lot. He did do a few photo spreads and a video with some guys a few years ago but it was before he really built up and he was blonde then so no one can prove it was him. Now he focuses on serious modelling, when he's not making people queue outside a half-empty club or posing for *International Male*.

"I go to the States in winter cos there's more body work out there—here it's all clothes and I'm too muscley for that ... sorry mate it's full you'll have to wait ... but over there you get loads of gym catalogs and swimwear and they really treat you with respect ... yeah fine Gavin go on up, Trish's waiting ... listen mate, I don't care if your friend's inside and you'll come straight out when you've given him a message, you'll have to wait ... so I was thinking of getting cheek implants like, to get more face work but my agent says it's not my face that everyone looks at. You know I want to be more than just a great body, I'm not just some beefy himbo ... 'scuse me miss, you do know this is a gay club, don't you?" ✶

The Boystown Gang

It can happen at any dance party. You're dancing your way through the crowd, people are smiling, laughing and kissing. The warmth, sweat and camaraderie fill you with love for the whole world. Suddenly the smiles disappear, the person-to-person contact vanishes and the temperature drops. You are in Boystown: a strange place inhabited by beautiful but unsmiling men. Take pity on this group. They are isolated by their perfection; no one ever dares approach them. Shunned through society's fickle rejection of body culture, they are forced to hang out together for comfort and support. You may feel they are attitude queens, refusing to acknowledge lesser beings but really they are just painfully shy. Despite having gym-honed bodies, being surrounded by other gorgeous men and being pumped with mood-enhancing chemicals (a condition which would render any normal gay man ecstatic in a touchyfeelygropey kind of way), they are unable to raise even a smile.

Grant is one such member of the Boystown Gang. A cruel childhood taught him to look good and say nothing. He has since been trapped in a vicious cycle of silently seeking approval through physical perfection. Please, if you stumble across him in Boystown, do not pass by—smile at him, kiss him, tell him how much you really, really love him. He may just sneer but deep inside a sad little boy will be grinning from ear to ear. ✶

The Martina Fan

Such is her devotion to the great Martina, Finn could be shown a pair of tennis knickers and accurately state in which Wimbledon final Martina wore them, what tennis skirt she wore, how many racquets she used and how many aces were served—all from the knickers.

Martina can do no wrong. Girlfriend trouble is always the partner's doing, and ghost-written novels are just a mature acknowledgment of her own limitations.

The hardest challenge was to justify her singing 'Living Doll' with Cliff Richard at a wet Wimbledon in 1996. The sight of Martina joining in the ultimate anthem of men's objectification of women with the writer and star of *Heathcliff! The Musical* and a committed Christian to boot almost brought a murmur to Finn's heart. That night she felt obliged to turn the Martina pillow face down when she went to bed.

After discussions with her support group and extensive role-playing of Martina in that situation, Finn finally understood the truth: worn down by years of unjust vilification as a miserable dyke and bad sport, Martina was trapped into a tokenistic display of heterosexually defined 'congeniality' by the

19

powerful coalition of the Wimbledon patriarchy, 5000 bored and angry social conservatives in a rain-drenched center court and the Anti-Dyke himself, Cliff Richard. She no doubt wept the bitter tears of humiliation on returning to her modest Montana cabin. Armed with this insightful analysis, Finn could once again turn the Martina pillow face up at night.

Any lingering doubts were soon swept aside by the Harley-Davidson trip across the U.S. "That's my girl," sighed Finn contentedly as she settled down to the Martina exercise tape one more time.

"One day I will do the exercises, but how can I concentrate on my inner thighs when hers are right in front of me?" ✶

Gay Man Trapped in a Lesbian Body

Claire first knew she wasn't like other girls when she went to a women's discussion group and discovered she was the only lesbian who was still using the name her parents gave her. She alone had not planned to go camping over Easter and she preferred watching *Hercules* to *Xena –Warrior Princess*. Sure Xena was sexy, but Hercules was just so camp!

Once she embraced her uniqueness, it took off: she refitted her kitchen and refuses to use the cooker, wears lycra, and drinks Cosmopolitans at a Philip Stark bar rather than beer at a pool table. She loves dancing with the boys in sweaty nightclubs, although she does have to wear a small plastic backpack and pretend to be a fag hag to get in, but that's a small price to pay to dance with your hands in the air and whoop.

Claire has taken it upon herself to bring gay male values to the lesbian world: she sleeps on the first date, she forgets names, she doesn't call and she thinks twenty minutes is a long session. Her best friends Mel, Jo and Chris are a little jealous of her pick-up skills in the toilets. "It takes us three hours and a case of beer to get sex, but all she has to do is wash her hands and she's away. It's just not fair." ✳

Photo Junkie

Troy is easily spotted: he's the one without his shirt, draped over two pretty muscle boys in the photo pages of the community press. However, the charming, slightly embarrassed, caught-by-surprise look is not easily achieved. Each week the papers have to be scoured to find where the photographers were last week and calculate where they will be this week. Then there's the agonizing wait for the photographer to turn up, the intensive 'pick me' thought transferal and that's only after you've found a few pretty guys to hang out with, buy drinks for and keep around until the time comes to flex the pecs and smile coyly.

Ideally, Troy will get caught at an early evening venue so he can enjoy the rest of the night without being in permanent pose. However, early evening shots do tend to be clothed, whereas shirtless shots score maximum points especially if taken in that fine borderline zone between relaxed-and-happy smile and totally-smashed leer at the camera.

Troy has yet to reach his ultimate goal: a color cover shot after White Party. Twelve hours of party, a dozen press photographers and one fabulous outfit—you'd think it would be easy, but there're 5,000 competitors and besides, just how many photos are taken in the men's toilets? *

Camp Dyke

A good fire is at the heart of a successful camping trip. No one knows this better than Jill—one of the world's keenest campers. None of your organized campsites with barbecues, toilet facilities and showers for her. If you're not in the woods with a three-hour trek to your car and the nearest electric power point then it's–just–not–camping. A tent, a sleeping bag and a light you can strap on your forehead are all you need. First Timers might require toilet paper as well.

Jill is always fire monitor when the girls go camping at Easter:

"No, no, no you have to grade the wood by thickness, one to seven. One is yer kindling, seven is yer log. You've got to build up your fire slowly from one to seven ... I think you'll find that wood's a little damp Bruce, put it here to dry. No not on the fire, you idiot. Who brought the bloody man—I don't want him buggering up my wood grading or he'll be banished to his tent, the gay-male-only space. Michelle you better check his guy ropes, see if he's done it properly. No, Bruce the beers go in the river to keep cool. No, there's no tonic for the vodka, besides we need the vodka to sterilize any wounds or animal bites. Now I'd say that stick's a three, put it in that pile there. Fun isn't it?" ✶

DJ Diva

DJs are rarely spotted beyond the murky apparition peering through the dry ice at the dance floor crowd, earphone askew on the head and one hand on the turntable. Early risers might catch Svate stumbling out of a taxi at 8 a.m., just getting home from a hard night's work, hallmark sunnies shielding her eyes from the morning light bouncing off her nose piercing. Her opinions and philosophies can often be read in street press DJ profiles:

"I've been overseas, playing a few sets in LA and London, a few gigs at Trade, DTPM which was a complete blast, the scene over there is just amazing now ... I really think it's important to take your crowd on a musical journey. I, like, get off on the idea that they end up dancing to something that would never make them walk onto a dance floor in the first place ... I think playing music people want to hear is a real bogus concept. I'm not there to give people easy options. Like if that's what you want just put in a jukebox and see how soon you get sick of Christina Aguilera ... At the moment I'm exploring a real jungle, drum and bass, techno thing with some wicked acid coming way out of left field in a really dark sexy sort of way—basically if you can sing it, I don't play it ... Influences: Danny Tenaglia cos he's just out there and Polywog cos she was just out there long before anyone else. At home? I listen to Loretta Lynn mainly. ✳

Rae and Rita-Mae are in a long-term relationship. They are inseparable. No one could imagine seeing one without the other —going for walks, playing in the park, sharing a lamb chop in front of *Wheel of Fortune*. They first met at the vet's; Rae was picking up some Pal professional formula for a friend when she saw Rita-Mae alone and whimpering – far from home, she was missing her family. Rae took her home, fed her, bathed her, cuddled her and wiped her mess from the carpet. They bonded.

Rae is a Drug Rehabilitation Counsellor and Rita-Mae is a Border Collie–Kelpie cross. They devote all their spare time to their life's work, a groundbreaking cookbook, *Dinner for Two: Meals to Share with Your Dog*. Rae carefully prepares dishes that fill the requirements of both canine and human nutrition and then they test them out on their friends: casseroles, sausages, roasts and even a few vegan dishes that Rita-Mae manages to force down to keep her loved one happy.

Both Rita-Mae and Rae are keen to start a family. However, of late, Rita-Mae has been rather more proactive in searching for a sperm donor and has chosen one of the more direct methods of insemination. Rae is looking for just one donor and even if this is the queer 90s he will be doing it the old fashioned way: a gay boy and a turkey baster. ∗

The Dog Lover

Domesticated Couple

Bernard and Crispin were wild party animals, determinedly contributing to the profits of bars, clubs and saunas like they were charitable institutions. They were aggressive singles that would snarl at the word monogamy until they met each other and a startling metamorphosis occurred:

"Oh we still go out, we're not one of those couples who get a dog and disappear out to the suburbs. Although the way house prices are going that's about all we're going to afford. We get out all the time—had a drink last Sunday. It's just the scene's really boring now, it's not that we've changed, but the The Pink Fit hasn't been the same since the remodeling ... well no, we can't go out tonight because we've got Kim and Lorraine round for dinner, but we can't stay up late because the parents are coming round tomorrow and we're all going to the House and Garden show before we head off to Aunty Irene and Uncle Frank's 30th. We are hoping to squeeze in a quick trip to Ikea because we think our new CD cabinet may have come in ... no, next weekend we've promised ourselves we're making the jams and pickles. It's the last chance we'll get before Christmas ... Black and Blue, is it that time already? Bet it's the same weekend we've booked to get the sofas steam cleaned. Don't know if we'll bother, it's not what it used to be, is it?" ✶

Foul-Mouthed Drag Queen

"Okay, let's hear it for our first-timer Chantella and her lovely rendition of 'I Will Always Love You' by Whitney Houston. Nice choice Chantella, she's like potty training for Drag Queens is Whitney, doesn't matter how much of a mess you make or how much you stink, everyone forgives you. Do that on a Diana Ross number and you're history.

"We'll be back with the main show in half an hour—that's if Fanny La Bouche isn't so pissed that she does her entire performance in the toilets again, wondering why no one's clapping. Still, she does do most of her performances in toilets around town. I'm sure you've all seen them, she probably forced you into a bit of audience participation too. I tell you, she's seen more cocks than a chicken farmer and the way her legs can snap shut, she's probably chopped more heads off too.

"So get your drinks at the bar. Don't get them off Richard— that's him, with tits bigger than me—he's a tight git with the vodka. Not so tight when it comes to giving head in the changing room are you Richard? We call him Red Cross because he gives so generously whenever someone knocks on his door ... Is it anyone's birthday today?" ∗

Ex-girlfriends always move to Byron Bay and manage cafés, as Kate found out on a trip there.

"It was awful," she said, "I went up there with Lisa and Michele to get away from it all only to find 'it' had all moved there before me and taken an espresso machine with it. I couldn't go in the first café because my ex Fran was there, who'd also slept with Michele and hated Lisa because she went out with Fran's girlfriend of six years after they broke up and before we started dating. The next café had Lisa's ex's best friend managing it, and she hated Lisa because she'd always loved the ex and blamed Lisa for keeping them apart even after they broke up. The next café was a total shock because Michele's supposed current who just disappeared along with the neighbours' car, only to call from Grafton saying she needed to find herself, was there handing out cappuccinos.

"There wasn't one café that all three of us could go into without one of us running into emotional baggage. In the end, we got takeaway lattés from separate places, braved polite conversation with each other's ex and tried to ignore the obvious attentions of the ex's current. We met on the beach to drink our coffees and look for dolphins to commune with, only to find my surfie chick heartbreaker riding in on a wave. And we thought Woodworking class was a minefield of past mistakes!" ✳

The Ex-Girlfriend

Fag Hag

Cheryl just loves gay boys—"they know how to have such a good time!" Gay boys are so friendly and accepting, "you can go to a gay club and there's no harassment and no attitude, everyone's just enjoying themselves". Cheryl is so used to being completely ignored in a straight venue that she thinks a bar where only fifty percent of the men cut her dead is an attitude-free zone.

Cheryl realized early in her gay career that the more outrageous she was and the more times she used the word *camp*, the more she could make the gay boys giggle so she turned up to the Beauchamp one night in a tiara, frilly dress and wings. "Now I'm a Fairy Queen too!"

Cheryl's best friend in the whole world is Gavin. They always go out together. He even tried to sneak her into a sauna. She got thrown out when a man groped her bum and she leapt up so fast her towel fell off and the next two minutes of *Acres of Ass* was projected onto her ample boobs.

Gavin keeps trying to persuade Cheryl she's a lesbian, but Cheryl doesn't think so—she doesn't like them very much as they're all too miserable. "I just love boys too much. Perhaps I'll have a sex change and be a gay man—what d'you reckon Gavin, we could be boyfriends then—it would be sooo camp!" ✶

The Gay Male Lesbian

Bruce's curse is that he is a man attracted to men and not a woman attracted to women, but what he cannot achieve sexually, he strives for socially. A perfect Sunday afternoon for him is coffee with all the girls, the same gang he spent Friday night with at Suzie's—"everyone bring a dish and we'll eat while we workshop what video we want to watch."

"It's tragic," said Craig, one of Bruce's former gay male friends. "One minute he was dancing with his shirt off at The Peel, the next he was off to garden centers looking for Australian natives to turn his back yard into a wilderness area ... I knew we should never have let him go on that camping trip over Easter with those girls. One weekend of outdoor life, building fires, gourmet cheese, six different pâtés and homemade olives and he was lost. Now he's stopped drinking vodka, taken to beer and allowed all his body hair to grow back. I fear for his health, I really do."

"I wouldn't mind," added Johnny, another concerned friend, "but they only want him for his sperm. Once they're impregnated he'll be tossed aside like a used husk and we'll be left to pick up the pieces, as per usual." ✶

Gorilla in the Mist

Paolo's hallmark is the faint whiff of eucalyptus disinfectant that he just doesn't seem to be able to get rid of. After so many hours lurking in steamy saunas, the smell seems to have permanently impregnated his skin and hangs around him like a vague memory of so many good times.

Such is the time Paolo has spent in the sauna that he has lost the ability to communicate verbally. However, his understanding of hand and body language would fill an anthropologist's notebook several times over. A quick nod of the head can mean, "get in here and into that sling if you know what's good for you," while a slight furrow of the brow communicates, "piss off, this spa's busy and we're not interested in having an old dog like you get off by perving on us".

At the sauna he has his own locker, a towel with his initials and a pigeonhole for messages—all rewards from their frequent sauna program. Another six visits and he'll be able to have his phone number embroidered on his towel too—not that phoning him is any good; when he answers the phone all he can do is raise his eyebrow and rub his crotch, leaving the caller thinking it's a faulty line. ✶

Granny Knows Best

The lovely thing about grandmothers is that they see nothing and know everything. Granny can sit through endless repeats of *Oklahoma* and *Carousel*, pat Franco's hand as he cries through Maria Von Trapp's wedding again, and think it's just lovely how young people today can appreciate the classics. She does wonder why she never hears Marco's motorbike when he arrives or leaves. He must have a motorbike—otherwise, why would he wear all those leather outfits?

For years now she's been asking him if he's met a special girl yet and every time he answers, "Granny, you know you're the only girl for me!" She likes to knit Franco jumpers—last birthday she gave him a lovely pullover with colored stripes. "I got the idea for it when you took me down Oxford Street and we met all those lovely biking friends of yours. You started chatting about all these girls you met at parties and what their flats looked like. Honestly, I never knew young men were so fussy about kitchen appliances. In my day men never stepped into a kitchen and now you spend hours talking about all manner of knobs and surfaces. Anyway, I saw all these things with rainbow stripes and thought 'how cheery', so I knitted this. Now, I've only used six colours because I couldn't get any indigo wool. I call it your freedom jumper because your granny knitted it for you and you should be proud to wear it wherever you like!" ✳

The Hair Stylist

"Look Francesca, love, I know Troy always did you a sundrenched auburn but I honestly feel your eyes are far more suited to the barleystraw gold. If I layer you at the back and raise you up here we can really feature your fabulous cheekbones. They're real aren't they—I can tell. People come in here and it doesn't matter who they've been done by, I just take one look in that mirror and know exactly what's been done. That mirror doesn't lie. When you look fabulous in there, you look fabulous period.

"All this surgery, it's not natural is it? It's not like hair, that's meant to be colored and styled, otherwise why would half the world have mousy brown mops? Dianne, you're supposed to be rinsing her, not drowning her ... Between you and me, she's not long for this studio. Strolls in as and when she likes—eleven o'clock this morning—'alarm didn't go off'. Didn't get to bed last night, more like.

"So we're going for the barleystraw gold then? Wise choice. Carl—love, can you finish off for me here, my 3:30's turned up and I can see her split ends from here. Francesca, love, Carl's going to take good care of you—he was top of his class at Community College. A bricklaying course, but I took one look at his hands and said 'you're wasted on bricks and mortar my boy, do my tinting'. He hasn't looked back since." *

45

Hollywood Queens

Michael and Stephen made the mistake of inviting Hollywood Queens round for dinner, and had their lives turned into a lurid black and white melodrama.

"What a dump, I've never been anywhere so filthy!"

"It's not you I'm angry with, darling, it's the dirt."

"Well what do you expect? She's nothing more than a common frump whose father lived over a grocery store and whose mother took in washing."

"Oh she's my very best friend, I wouldn't harm her for the world. But have you seen what she's wearing?"

"Yes, someone should take her upstairs and remove that dog of a dress."

"You'll never guess who we saw at the sauna, you'll die darling, you'll simply die—Stephen. I shan't be able to look at Michael all dinner."

"Wouldn't it be awful, wouldn't it be ghastly, eating his food and knowing all about his husband ..."

"But what if Michael finds out?"

"Well we'll just have to fasten our seatbelts cause it's gonna be a bumpy night."

"Well I saw it coming, I said to Michael, 'Mary Haines, you're living in a fool's paradise', but the silly fool won't watch a film unless Jean-Claude Van Damme drops his pants in it so he didn't have a clue what I was talking about!" ✳

47

House Hunters

David and Andrew spend their Saturdays viewing property. They do have their own home but love the excitement of viewing houses and taking peeks into other people's lives.

"Queens—as per Clinique in the bathroom, Mardi Gras CD in the living room and that god-awful muscle man holding the tires in the bedroom."

"One of them's a Qantas steward—priority luggage tag on the suitcase above the wardrobe."

"One's fat—Linda Evangelista Treadmill and enough Cadbury wrappers in the bin to paper the second bedroom."

"Possible bulimic—multipacks of toilet paper and a picture of Diana on the fridge."

"Of course, one flies off round the world all the time, the other binges on chocolate, sees Diana on the fridge while reaching for the Homer Hudson, leaps on the treadmill for some fast and furious before a tonsil tickle in the bathroom ..."

"... Went to therapy, new self, fresh start, break up, put the house on the market, fight over the Liz Taylor biography I saw torn in two on the landing. Now, who?"

"That couple that were at Stewart and Bill's for dinner. They lived in this area, one was a steward ..."

"... and the other wolfed down the dessert—it's them. Right, where next?" ✶

The Vile Beaches

The beach is a great leveller in the gay community as no one, however perfect his body might be, goes without the esteem-destroying scrutiny of the public-spirited vile beaches. They lie in packs, the whole beach covered by their microscopic gaze. Going for a swim at their beach is dangerous. You can get bruised, scratched, battered and torn to shreds ... just from their comments. The only comfort is that their greatest vileness is preserved for those more beautiful than themselves.

"Mmm, looks like Hugh went to Silicon City and brought back a couple of souvenirs for his chest. Those pecs appeared faster than Lonnie Gordon at a gay pride benefit."

"Look at Grant—he's been getting a bit of help working out at the gym, GEARing up for summer. His thighs are huge! Why bother, when his ankles look like they'll snap under the weight?"

"Gavin must have found a lover, one who likes a few love handles to hold on to."

"Puh-lease, the only long-term lover he's ever had is Sara Lee, and believe me, that's a lifetime commitment."

The only interruption to the noble social service they provide is the ring of a mobile:

"Ya ... oh hi Craig ... just relaxing at the beach, oblivious to the world. Bob Paris himself could walk past, and I wouldn't notice a damn thing—except did you see that photo of him in *Genre*? Couldn't call that aging gracefully, could you?" ✳

Leather Queen

Franco can be found lurking at the Barracks, the Laird, the Anvil or any aggressive-sounding place. The chaps, leather jacket, cockring and shaved hair are a mean look but do not be deceived, he could just as well whip you up a fabulous spinach soufflé as whip you up.

The range of appliances in Franco's bedroom is matched only by the range of appliances in his kitchen and there is considerable crossover. "After what he did with the spaghetti spoon while in the sling, all I could think was, thank God we ate beforehand," said one of Franco's intimate dinner guests.

He might dole out some mean punishment in the bedroom, but it's nothing compared to the hard time the kitchen scourer gets. He does employ a cleaner, but he's so house-proud that the only way you can tell she's been is that one of the cups is facing the wrong way. The glass coffee table is smudge free and hosts six strategically placed black rubber coasters, a tidy pile of *Blue* magazines and a spotless ancient Javanese fertility god. The bookcase contains the works of Tom of Finland and the music of Rogers and Hammerstein, both in alphabetical order.

His fantasy man is a well-douched hairy-chested top who can be paddled into submission while singing 'Some Enchanted Evening'. Franco has yet to meet this man. ✷

Try-Hard Father

I suppose it did take some time to adjust when our Noeline came home with Lesley. I'm meant to call her Noel now but she'll always be little Noeline to me. First I just didn't get it—I mean, what do they actually do? Have they got the necessary parts? But then I thought it was better than some rough bastard doing my little girl in a panel van. I used to hide in the garage when Lesley came round—reckoned it was safe, but then she follows me in one day with a couple of beers. Next thing I know she's under the bonnet of the Commodore asking for an adjustable spanner. Must say the car's never run better and that lawn mower finally works again after that bastard from next door buggered it. Mum keeps going on about her lovely new kitchen cupboard and how the washing machine doesn't leak anymore.

"Next thing I know, she's sitting beside me when the cricket's on and buggered if she doesn't know every Australian lineup since 1954.

"I always wanted Noeline to marry a plumber or a carpenter because it would be really useful, but you've got to hand it to our girl, she's landed every bloody craftsman rolled into one woman. How do they learn all those bloody skills? Where do they get the time? That must be what they do in bed—sit up reading car manuals and carpentry books for hours on end." ✶

Muscle Mary

There is a sensible rule in the gay and lesbian community: never get into the back of a car with a Muscle Mary two months before a dance party. If the acrid stench of the steroid gym sweat doesn't knock you out, the 'roid rage over who knocked his gym gloves off the seat probably will. Should a fart be emitted, the safety of all passengers is at risk.

This is peak building up time for Muscle Mary, when the only prick that gets near his bum has a syringe full of chemicals attached. The spots are competing with the back hair for skin surface and everyone around him keeps pissing him off!

The journey home from the gym is peak protein consumption time so the hard boiled eggs are out even before the seat belts are fastened. The conversation is a set-by-set account of his workout and a detailed discussion on how to grill skinless chicken breasts with maximum taste and minimum fat:

"Right now I'm cutting up—building mass which I can then sculpt down to my target physique. I really blasted those rear delts today. I think they'll give the symmetry and maturity I'm looking for in my finished form ... get that protein shake from my bag ... right now, definition's not an issue but come September 3rd I start my cutting down, it's gonna be definition all the way ... I'll have that tin of tuna now .... d'you reckon I should coat the chicken in amino acid powder before or after I grill it?" ✳

Personal Trainer

The gyms frequented by the gay and lesbian community are full of body management professionals committed to excellence in helping people to achieve their health and fitness goals:

"I couldn't believe it when they took *Gladiators* off the air. I was this close to being one of the gladiators. I'd passed the audition ... c'mon rep it out, mate ... and they had shortlisted names for me. I was gonna be Thor, Vulture, Panther or Pickaxe ... keep your elbows back, mate ... I liked Panther, but Natalie the production assistant assigned to me, said something about terrorists which I didn't get. She liked Vulture ... okay rest ... but my mum reckoned it wasn't a good role model for kids cos vultures prey on the dead ... off you go, another set, pump it this time, mate ... didn't bloody know what Thor meant, sounds like a broken fridge to me so we were left with Pickaxe which I reckon would've been okay like, cos they use them in building so it's like powerful ... sorry mate didn't see you struggling there ... but constructive which is a good image for the kids. Don't know why they axed it, it was great ... okay you're done, great workout mate, that'll be $50, thanks." ✱

Prospecting Mothers

Jo and Natasha were the most separate of lesbian separatists until the demands of procreation forced them to change their ways. Suddenly they were hanging around gay boy haunts—the gym, the beach, bars and shops—discovering skills they never thought they had, such as eyeing-off men like seasoned old slut queens:

"Mmm, his chest's not bad and his shoulders are good but his legs are too skinny. Look at those calves! That's genetic and I'm not having a child of ours with chicken legs."

"But his eyes are really nice, Natasha, and they'd go great with your eyebrows."

They'd discretely browse potential donors to begin their character assessments: "He seems intelligent enough—I heard him talking about court. He might be a lawyer."

"Actually I think he's a drag queen, he said court shoes, not court room ... That guy in the blue Speedos is writing—perhaps he's an author or something creative."

"No, it's a personal ad – I can see 'no fats or fem's."

If that stage necessitated some difficult activities then the next involved even greater compromises. Dashing across town in a taxi with a sample jar kept at body temperature in the armpit. Getting stuck in traffic by Centennial Park and sprinting in there for an emergency insemination followed by a fifteen minute headstand against a tree to help speed the going. When that failed, the Gertrude Stein memorial spare room had to be converted into a male donation chamber. This led to the humiliation of being caught in the sex shop by their Womens Literature Discussion Group facilitator. She was complaining about the lack of non-male focused dildos while they were flicking through *Honcho*, *Colt* and the *Abercrombie and Fitch* catalogue for donor inspiration material.

Conception itself led to even more sacrifices: swapping the *Practical Carpentry* subscription for Practical Parenting, and downing power drills to take up knitting. ★

Tag Fag

1997 was not a good year for Jonathan—the tragic death of Versace had him in tears and wearing black for a month. Fortunately Gianni himself managed to help with a steady stream of gorgeous black items, as if eerily designing mourners for his own funeral. Secretly, it was a relief for Jonathan to have an excuse not to wear the multicolored eruptions which constituted the rest of his Versace collection.

Barely was Jonathan back into the muted darker colors of the season when Diana's tragic accident plunged him into a new abyss: "We were ninth cousins, you know. Gianni was the loss of a mentor but this is much too close to home, it's a very personal loss."

Since then Jonathan has lurched from designer to designer, Issy to Georgio, Donna K to Nicole Fahri and, in the height of his confusion, even stumbling into a pair of Banana Republic chocolate brown chinos. He still hasn't found his look—Donnatella was a pale shadow, and brought back too many sad memories. A sad figure, Jonathan sits in his underwear at home, flicking through *The Face* and *Vogue* in the forlorn hope of seeing some clothes he could stand to wear and praying for the good health of Calvin Klein, lest he be stripped of his final vestiges of dignity. ✶

The Travel Agent

Lynne has been showing overseas gay boys how to have a good time in Australia for years now. Shunting them through the hotel from Priscilla, onto the Priscilla Shopping Tour, the Priscilla Koala Patting Experience and finishing off with a few days in Cairns for Muriel's Tropical Paradise Experience:

"Sorry, sweetheart, don't do trips for girls. Tried it a couple of years back—got a few decent shags but far too much bloody hard work. Gay boys are easy—show 'em a drag queen, give 'em a stripper, point them at the nearest bathhouse, they love you to bits and don't care how much they pay. Don't need fabulous hotel rooms cos they never spend a night there. But the girls! Gawd, they want trips, theater, art, discussion groups and a wide range of lesbian venues—talk about asking for the impossible. Can't fob them off with a quick tour round the suburbs in a clapped out old coach to the tune of 'I Love the Nightlife.' Every coach trip I did for them started late because they had to reach consensus on what music got played before we set off.

"No love, I'll stick to the boys—they may get their dicks out for the pass-out stamp at the Welcome Night Drinks Party, but at least I don't have to spend $500 putting butcher's paper and marker pens in every room." ✳

Mardi Gras Board Member

Jem joined the Board of Sydney Gay & Lesbian Mardi Gras (SGLMG) because she wanted to make friends and gain social acceptance. After all, no one wants to know you when you're a photocopier repair person, unless they've got some paper jammed in their scanning drum. She knew she'd achieved the goal of becoming a prominent community member when she was finally featured in the gossip column of *Sydney Star Observer*: "Which Mardi Gras Board Member was seen rolling down the steps of Gilligans shouting 'But I'm on the Board of Mardi Gras, you've got to let me in'?" She thought it was about her, but then so many of the Board had rolled down those very steps.

Jem can be seen running around proudly at the Mardi Gras Party in her special red BOARD MEMBER T-shirt. Round Jem's neck on a bright pink rope are a stack of magnificent security passes: Board Card, Guest Bar Pass, Crew, Performer and Access All Areas —only the president could have more. She admits the AAA is the only one she needs, but who would take her seriously if she only had one card hanging round her neck?

This party is the most exhilarating of Jem's life. Okay, she may not be dancing with hundreds of topless beauties, and some might say snorting a line of speed before four hours of coat-check duty is a waste, but thousands of party-goers depend on Jem to store their rucksacks properly. It is an awesome responsibility. ✳

Receptionist From Hell

Mike is a switch bitch and proud of it. His never-fail hangover cure is to spend a morning answering the phone just as someone walks up to reception and starts speaking.

"Good morning, I'm looking for ..."

"National AIDS Federation, how may I help you? I'll see if he wants to speak to you—who is it? Sorry no answer, bye ... yes, I can take a short message ... yes, I know, all the messages we take are extremely important. Bye. Bitch. Yes, how may I help you?"

"I'm looking ..."

"N.A.F.O.A., how may I help you? ... not back 'til Friday, bye."

"I'm loo ..."

"N.A.F.O.A., how may I help you? ... aw, Gavin, hi darls, how are you? It's been non-stop all morning. I was only supposed to be on 'til eleven but apparently Paolo's sick ... yes, he seemed pretty healthy when Grant saw him leaving the tubs last night ... yes of course he was there again. Grant swears Paolo left with that guy that stalked Greg, you know the one that phoned him the following day, sent a poem to his home and turned up at his work with those roses ... I know, creepy isn't it! Paolo's probably being chased round the kitchen table with a carving knife right now. Look I've got to go, there's this miserable bugger pacing round reception. See ya darl ... Yes, how may I help you?"

"I was looking for Paolo. I just wanted to leave these roses for him." ✳

The Facilitator

"My name is Bronwyn and I'm not here in any sort of 'leadership' or 'educator' role—I have as much to learn today as anyone else. I'm just here to facilitate. Now this is only a one-day workshop but I think we can explore some really useful areas.

"First we need to establish a set of rules. It's important that we all have ownership of these so we'll operate on a consensus model. That should take us up to morning tea. Herbal teas and Ecco are available, and you'll have to go outside for a smoke.

"After tea we'll move on to some group-building exercises and then we should look at what our hopes, fears and expectations of the workshop are. From there we'll be able to write up what our group objectives are. That should take us to lunch.

"After lunch we'll recap and then we'll each check our own expectations and look collectively at whether we are achieving our group objectives. By that stage, we might be a bit tired so we'll do a few energy building games. That'll lead into afternoon tea.

"Once that's over we can move into evaluating the course and doing some closure activity. I think its important to have a sense of completion as a group. Okay?

"So to get the ball rolling, as it were, I want whoever catches this ball to say their name then throw the ball to someone else. My name's Bronwyn ..." ✳

The Accepting Mother

Mike thought he was delivering a killer blow to his mother when he decided to come out by bringing his boyfriend, Steve, home for the weekend. Imagine his horror when instead of outrage she declared:

"Oh, we've known all along, I'm so pleased you finally told us, my counsellor at the support group said you'd come round on your own eventually—I just had to give you some time to get used to the idea. Now I've put you two in the guest room as the bed's bigger, there's condoms and lube in a hand-painted Mexican bowl and a few toys and things in the drawer—make as much noise as you want, the walls are quite thick. Now, Steve, I'm sure you'd like to see pictures of Mike when he was a baby … Mike don't be silly of course he does … here he is when he tried to cut his own hair, doesn't he look cute. See I knew he'd be a hairdresser, even then. I'm sure you've noticed that pout he gives when he's not getting his own way—yes just like the one he's giving now. Well I always find it best to ignore it completely, don't you? Come into the kitchen, Steve, and we can really get to know each other. I just know we're going to get on so well." ✳

The Aerobic Instructor

The Aerobic Instructor's mission in life is to vent all his unrealized dance ambitions on unsuspecting exercisers. While eager athletes may think they are at the gym to exercise bodies and switch off minds, the instructor knows he's there to drag them through a routine that makes the Riverdance choreography look like hopscotch. After the torture of dragging newcomers out of the closet it's straight into the coded language designed to make novices feel inferior:

"Anyone here for the first time? Yes—you behind the pillar in the baggy shorts—go at your own pace but try to keep up. Okay let's work! It's only six weeks to Mardi Gras. Give me an L-shaped grapevine, turn, easy walk, turn, sidekick, shuffle and double time."

You may retreat to the seeming simplicity of the step class (what could be simpler than standing on and off a box?) but he's waiting there to torment you further:

"Okay give me a U step, reverse V, three knee repeaters, round the world, indecision and T step, and let's do it without me having to take you through the steps this time and don't forget over the rainbow with those arms!" *

Attitude Queen

The Attitude Queen's mission in life is to shoot everything down in flames. Fads, fashions, ideas, passions—they are all dead wood which need to be cut out of his life.

70s Revival: "Puh-lease, does the revival really need to last longer than the decade?"

Goatee Beards: "The Stonewall just looks like an alpine slope: full of goats swilling down their Stoli and tonics."

Bisexuality: "Fine, until I realized I'd have to sleep with Leanne as well as her boyfriend to qualify."

Muscle Marys: "Puh-lease, if I'm going to inject drugs I'd rather whack up something far more mood enhancing."

Loving Your Body As It Is: "Well, if that's your attitude you may as well, because no one else will."

Heroin Chic: "When I'm dead just toss a few rags on my corpse and then perhaps I'll finally make it into *The Face*."

Tattoos: "It's all very well, but what happens when 'Love', 'Hate' and Celtic armbands go out of fashion?"

Lounge Music: "If I'd wanted to sit around and listen to Dean Martin, I'd have stayed with my parents."

Attitude: "Puh-lease, over it—when am I going to be able to buy a Caffe Latte in this town without the waiter's face souring the milk?" ✳

Gay Shop Assistant

No one knows the truth of the term 'sex sells' like Chris and the other boys that work in gay shops. So what if the greasy old blokes grope your bum on their way to the tasteful male nude photography as you're stacking the bottom shelf for the tenth time this morning—"Whatever makes the sale" is Chris's cheery catch-cry as he swipes the gold Amex for another $200 purchase:

"You're right, I'm not wearing any underwear, how could you tell? You weren't looking, were you? No, that's not my only tattoo, but I'm not showing you the other one—not in public anyway. Outrageous! I do have a boyfriend you know ... now how are you going on there in the changing room ... yeah you look really sexy in that, your bum looks great. No! No such thing as too tight ... if you've got it, flaunt it—and in that, it looks like you have plenty of 'it'! Now there's an offer, if only I was single—come back next week, I might be ... did I say that last week? Oh well, we live in hope. Fabulous, that'll be $235 thank you ... that sounds fun but I'm busy tonight, besides my boyfriend wouldn't be too pleased ... sorry, we don't do threesomes." ✳

Serial Sugar Daddy

Sugar Daddy has it all: money, wealth and a platinum Amex. He knows these are all he needs to get all he wants in life. He bought the best body his body type could afford from Brett his personal trainer, just 500 easy payments of $150 a week. His tan is flown in from Hawaii during winter and topped-up on the world's most advanced sunbed. His relaxed demeanor comes courtesy of his masseur, herbalist and therapist, and the glamour supplied by his speed boat on the harbor. The current boyfriend comes courtesy of platinum Amex—spend more than $100,000 per annum and receive a new 21-year-old every three years.

Sugar Daddy has a pack of acolytes who hang on his every dollar. They are ex-boyfriends not silly enough to write themselves completely out of the picture, aspiring boyfriends, or guys who know a good thing when they see it. When Sugar Daddy wants a good time with his friends, they line up and recite their catechism—"you're looking fantastic ... you're looking so young ... I would die for that shirt it's fabulous," and they receive communion—usually an ecstasy tablet. The acolytes are useful; they serve to remind the current boyfriend that several came before him, more want to come after, and should he ever get lost, Amex can have a replacement there within 24 hours. ✳

The Folk Singer

Joni Mitchell without the sense of humour" read the review of Caye's performance in *Lesbian Folk* newsletter. It was a proud moment. Caye came to singing late—after years of crying over 'Court and Spark.' Caye finally realized that Joni was singing about her own experiences. She had not, in fact, astrally projected into Caye's life and used it for source material. It was a sad but rewarding moment; the end of Caye's intense relationship with Joni but the beginning of Caye's relationship with herself. Now she would voice her own pain rather than live through someone else's. She would express herself through songs such as 'Broken Woman' and 'Every Day I Bleed,' and her signature empowerment anthems 'Warrior Goddess' and 'The Woman She Is a Mountain.'

Having written the songs and applied for development funding, Caye set about learning the guitar. She chose not to go the traditional male-centric play-in-a-day, guitar-as-phallic-conquest route but rather to learn with Joni's help. This was where her years of listening finally paid off—her intimate knowledge of all Joni's arrangements meant Caye was able to recreate the chords just by experimenting with her guitar. She could feel the hand of Joni guiding her, a constructive positive synergy, mentor helping novice to find her own voice. ✶

The Window Dresser

George has been doing ISDs (In Store Displays) and SVDs (Street Visible Displays) for seven years and he is a visual merchandiser—not a window dresser. His attempt to debunk the cruel, camp, stereotypical image of visual merchandisers is challenged by his insistence that a wrist-mounted pin cushion is a necessity and by his genetically programmed need to ruche fabric. Now he has a major Nina Ricci promotion to coordinate.

"I don't want to see any pastels. I want flags all the way down the central cosmetics aisle right up to the Estee Lauder gondola, okay? I want the GWP scarves billowing (that's 'Gift With Purchase', Colin) but not blasting—we're a spring breeze, not a tornado. I don't want to see any wilting flowers. These halogen downlights are fierce, so—Connie—I want you to replace the flowers daily, twice for late-night shopping. I want cloths over the display tables. Layered, Colin! Harmony Purple, Fireball Orange, Harmony Purple and 'nearest match' isn't good enough. You've got the sample so stick to it. I don't want to see any Very Violet 'because it's pretty close'. Suzanne, start on the signage—I want to see bold lettering with a feminine edge, our Nina Ricci woman is strong but yielding, so I want our consonants to be the same. I'm off to the check the Statue of Liberty fruit installation. Connie, you've got the pin cushion, you're in charge." ✳

Workshop Junkie

ife changed for Miranda when she went on her 'Unleashing the Goddess Within' workshop. She realized she was Hecate, queen of witches. She knew this was a turning point: "When you've bled into a mound of earth that you've dug yourself in the middle of the forest by the light of a full moon, you know you'll never be the same again."

After the Goddess workshop, Miranda/Hecate spent two days in the Dandenongs learning to love her breasts. Then she took the poem she wrote to her breasts and turned it into an interpretative dance.

Since discovering in her 'Past Lives, Future Guidance' correspondence course that she was a persecuted lesbian nun in 14th century Spain, she has defined her sexuality as "empathetic celibate lesbian", or in the words of Mel at the 'Small Holes and Dangly Bits: Exploring Sexuality With Child-Like Joy' workshop, "a pseudo-lezzo clit-tease."

Stung by that unsolicited negative feedback, Miranda/Hecate sought to resolve her own issues through 'Defining Selves' which used techniques of psycho-drama, psycho-song, psycho-sand-play and mask therapy. Through various role play situations she discovered what was really missing in her life was Jesus. Her heart opened and the light shone in, banishing Hecate and replacing her with a need to dress badly and look really clean. ✳

"We had to completely refloor the living area simply because c the knobs on the cooker," announced Richard the accountant.

"It was a nightmare," added his boyfriend, Colin the lawye "we had to refit the kitchen. It was looking very early 90s an we couldn't stand Ross and Phil upstairs bragging about thei Poggen Pohl kitchen. We used Trevor's carpenter because he wa supposed to be a real spunk. Either we got his overweight fathe or Trevor's sexual tastes need exploring with a therapist ..."

"After weeks of noise, mess and no fantasy-workman-sex, w had the new kitchen, except the cooker knobs were all wrong You can't just replace them so Colin insisted on a whole nev cooker."

"Well, we knew how to operate this one and I always say b the time you work out how to use the cooker, it's out of date."

"So, beautiful Smeg appliance installed, 300 pages o instructions and the kitchen's perfect. Only, the cutlery doesn match and we see this fantastic canteen in *Vogue Living*. Thre months to get them shipped over from Finland."

"Fell in love with this table, except the glass top reveal Trevor's dirty great red wine stain."

"So the carpet had to go—the polished wood goes better witl glass—and we found this fantastic bouncy rubber-backed stuf But now the problem is the bathroom—it looks so old!" ✳

Yuppie Queens